Grocery Store Workers

Julie Murray

Abdo Kids Junior
is an imprint of Abdo Kids
abdobooks.com

Abdo
Kids

MY COMMUNITY: JOBS

abdobooks.com

Published by Abdo Kids, a division of ABDO, P.O. Box 398166, Minneapolis, Minnesota 55439.
Copyright © 2021 by Abdo Consulting Group, Inc. International copyrights reserved in all countries.
No part of this book may be reproduced in any form without written permission from the publisher.
Abdo Kids Junior™ is a trademark and logo of Abdo Kids.

Printed in the United States of America, North Mankato, Minnesota.

102020

012021

 THIS BOOK CONTAINS
RECYCLED MATERIALS

Photo Credits: iStock, Shutterstock

Production Contributors: Teddy Borth, Jennie Forsberg, Grace Hansen

Design Contributors: Candice Keimig, Dorothy Toth

Library of Congress Control Number: 2020910591

Publisher's Cataloging-in-Publication Data

Names: Murray, Julie, author.

Title: Grocery store workers / by Julie Murray

Description: Minneapolis, Minnesota : Abdo Kids, 2021 | Series: My community: jobs | Includes online
        resources and index.

Identifiers: ISBN 9781098205829 (lib. bdg.) | ISBN 9781098206383 (ebook) | ISBN 9781098206666
        (Read-to-Me ebook)

Subjects: LCSH: Grocery trade--Juvenile literature. | Grocery shopping--Juvenile literature. | Community
        life--Juvenile literature. | Occupations--Juvenile literature. | Cities and towns--Juvenile literature.

Classification: DDC 381.41--dc23

Table of Contents

Grocery Store Workers

The grocery store is open!

Many people work there.

Sue works in the bakery.

She makes baked goods.

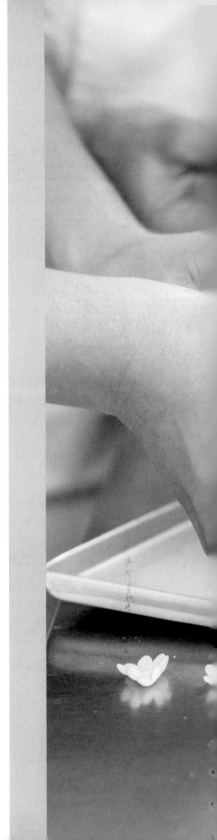

Dani has red apples. She places them on the table.

Larry works in the
deli. He helps Fay.

11

Liz **stocks** the shelves.

She lines up the jars.

Evan is a cashier.

He scans the items.

Liam bags the food.

Erin cleans the store. She uses a big floor scrubber!

19

Todd works outside.

He collects the carts.

A Grocery Store Worker's Tools

carts

cash register

cleaning supplies

food

Glossary

deli
a store or area in a store where ready-to-eat foods, deli meats, and cheeses are sold.

stock
to keep ready for sale.

Index

MAY 2021